Beauty and Nature Portrait Collection

By Kelly Horton

I0503809

Copyright 2018 Kelly Horton

ALL RIGHTS RESERVED

For any further details, including information on other books or colouring pages contact:

Kellyartistthorton@yahoo.com

For more colouring pages:

www.etsy.com/uk/Colourcollectiveshop

Join the Facebook Community: Search for the

The Colouring Collective

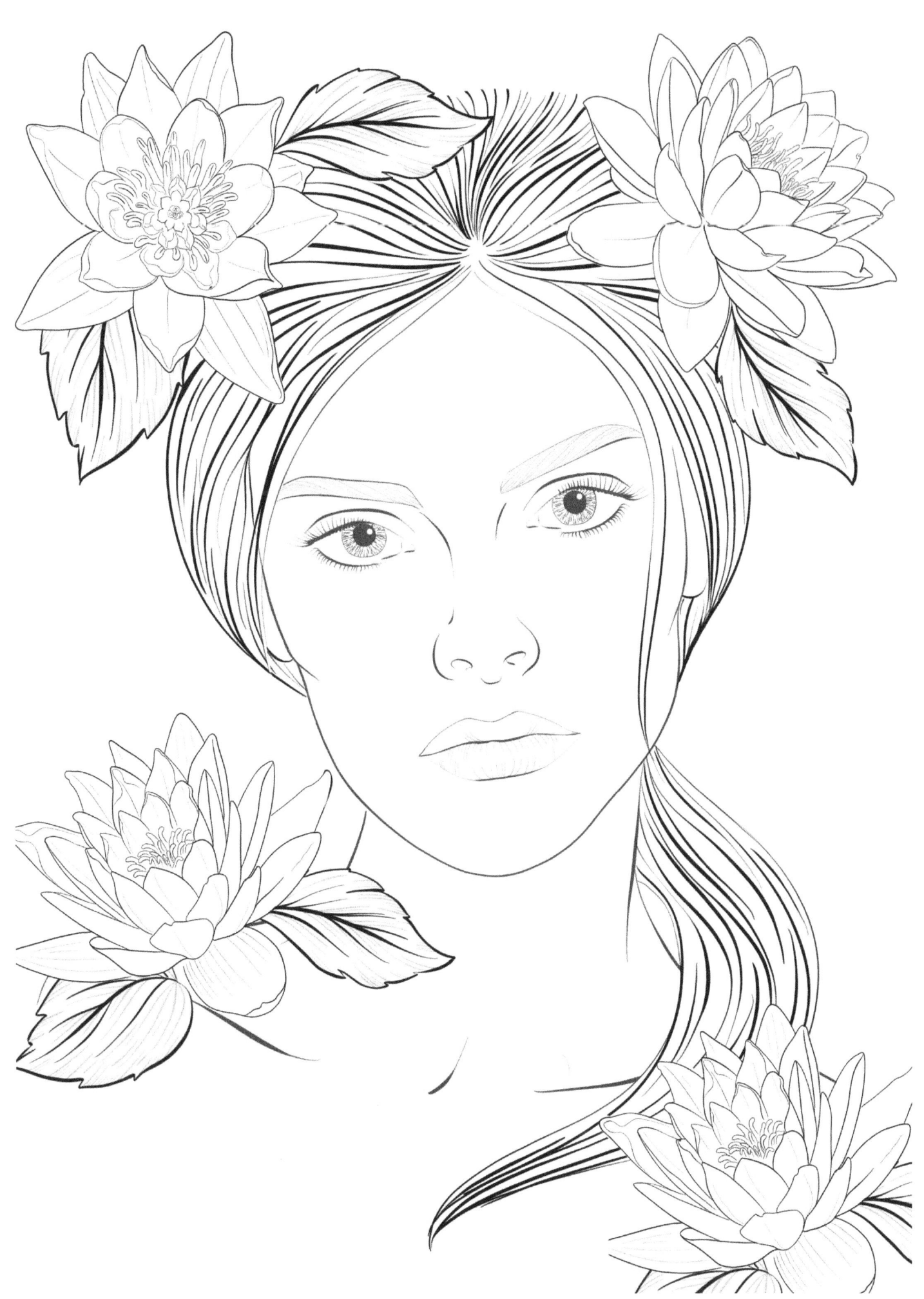

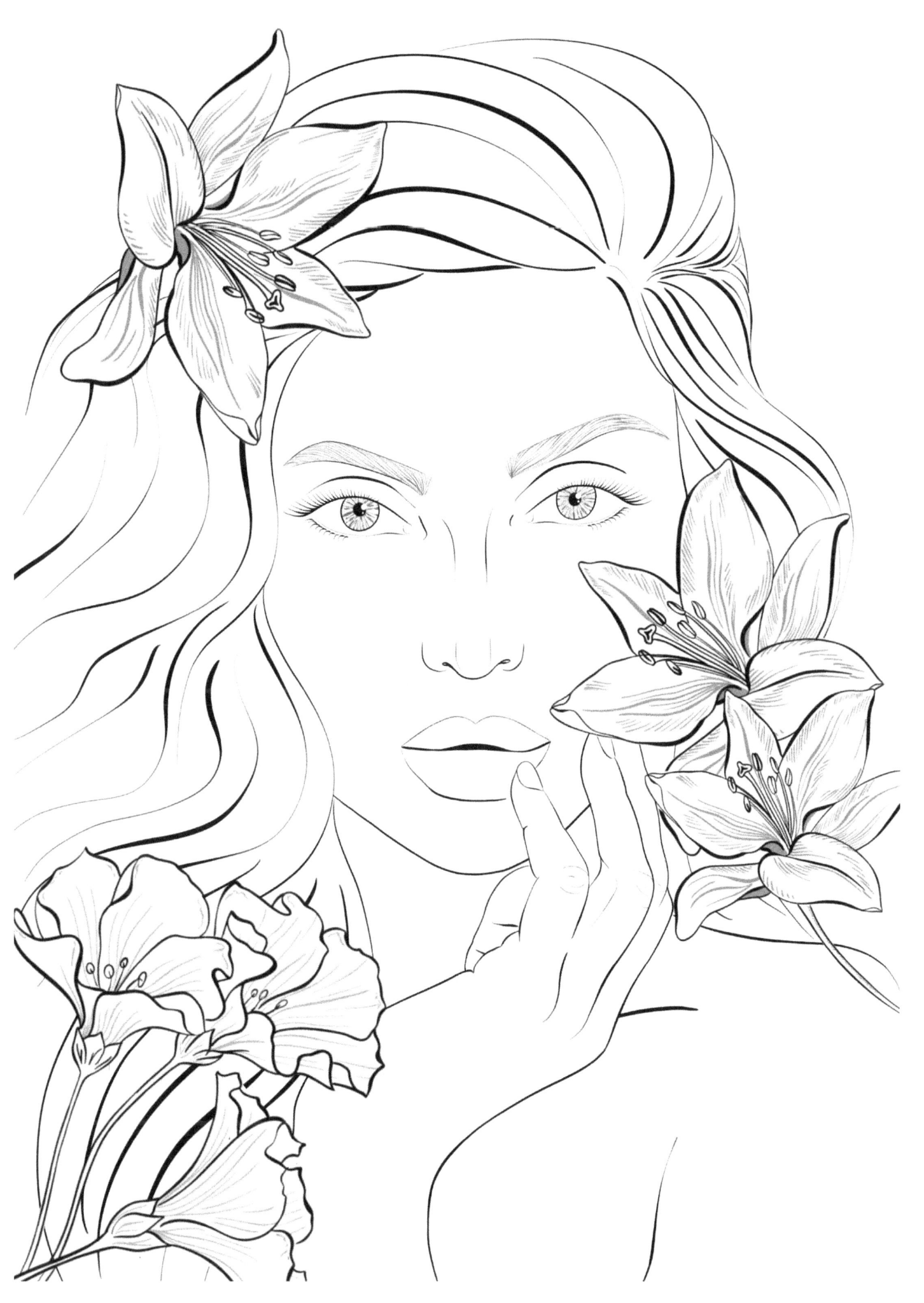

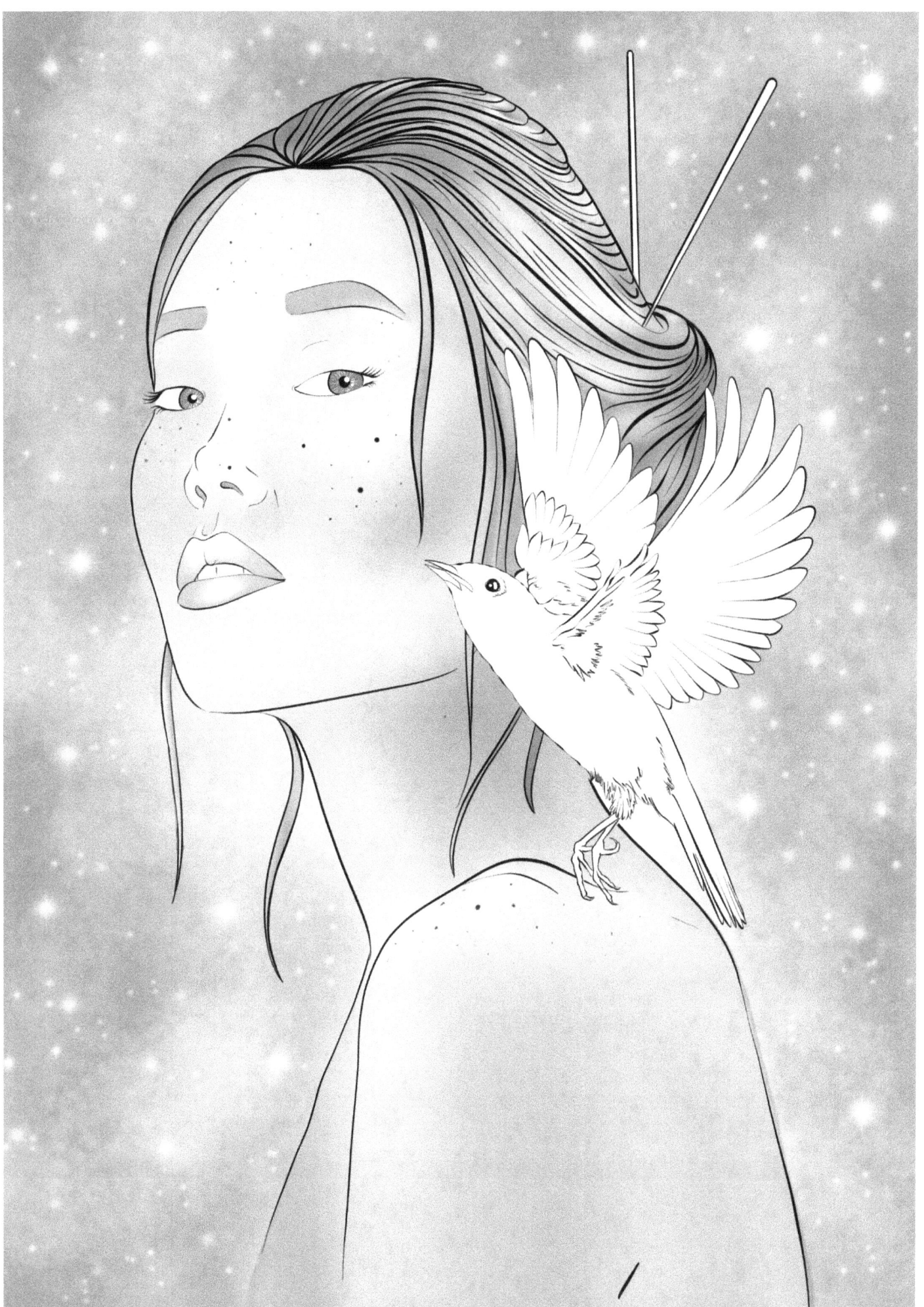

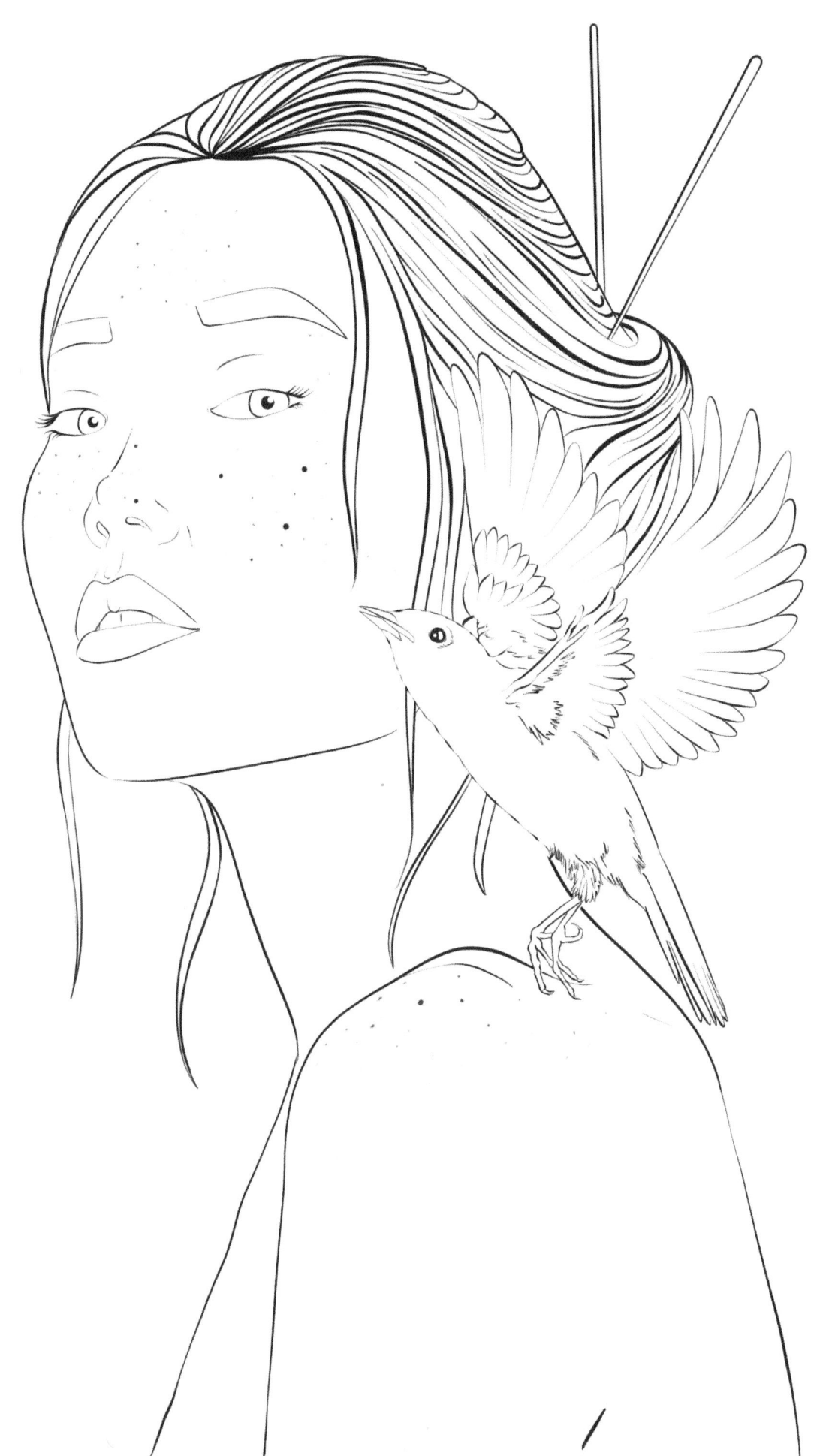

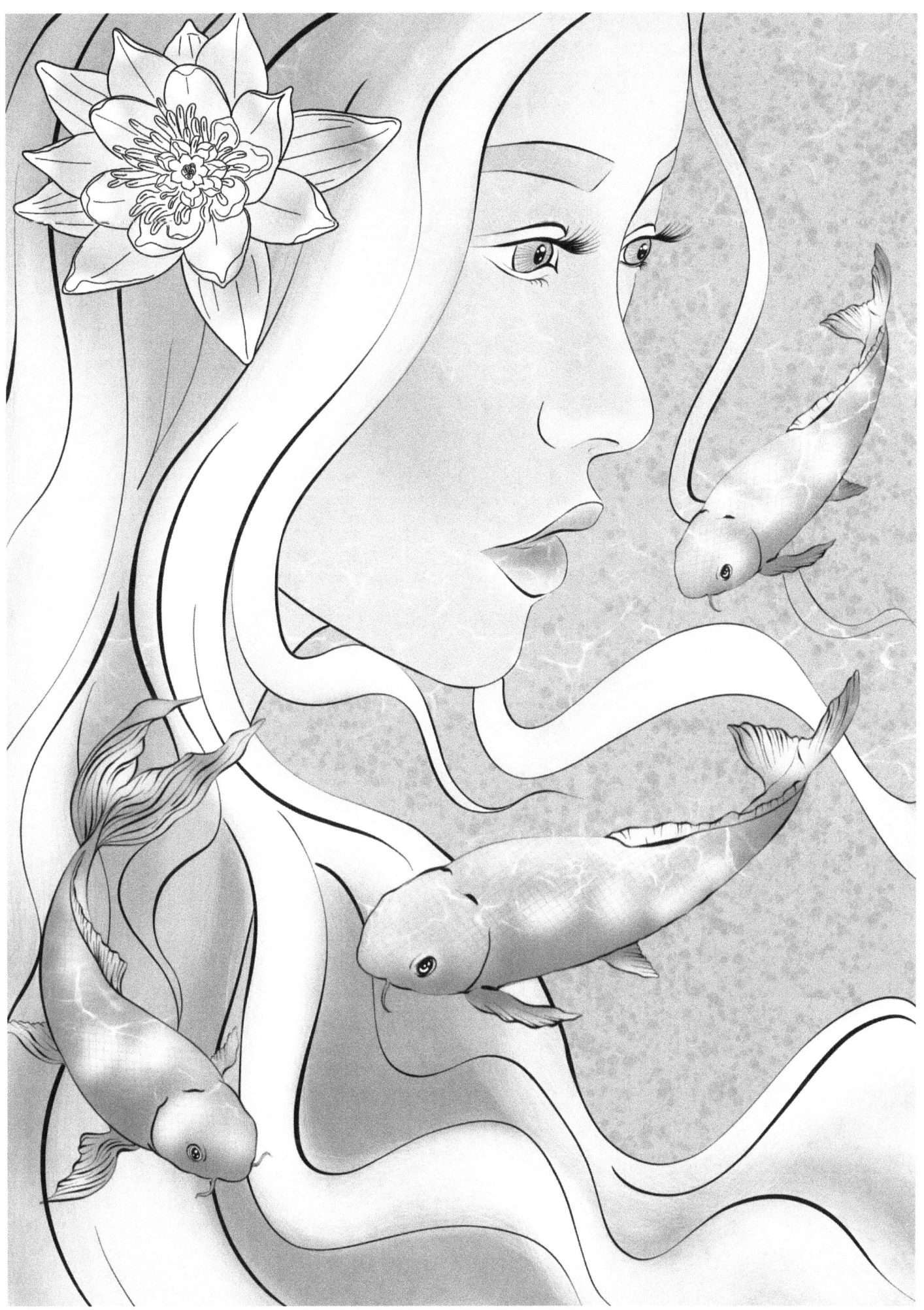

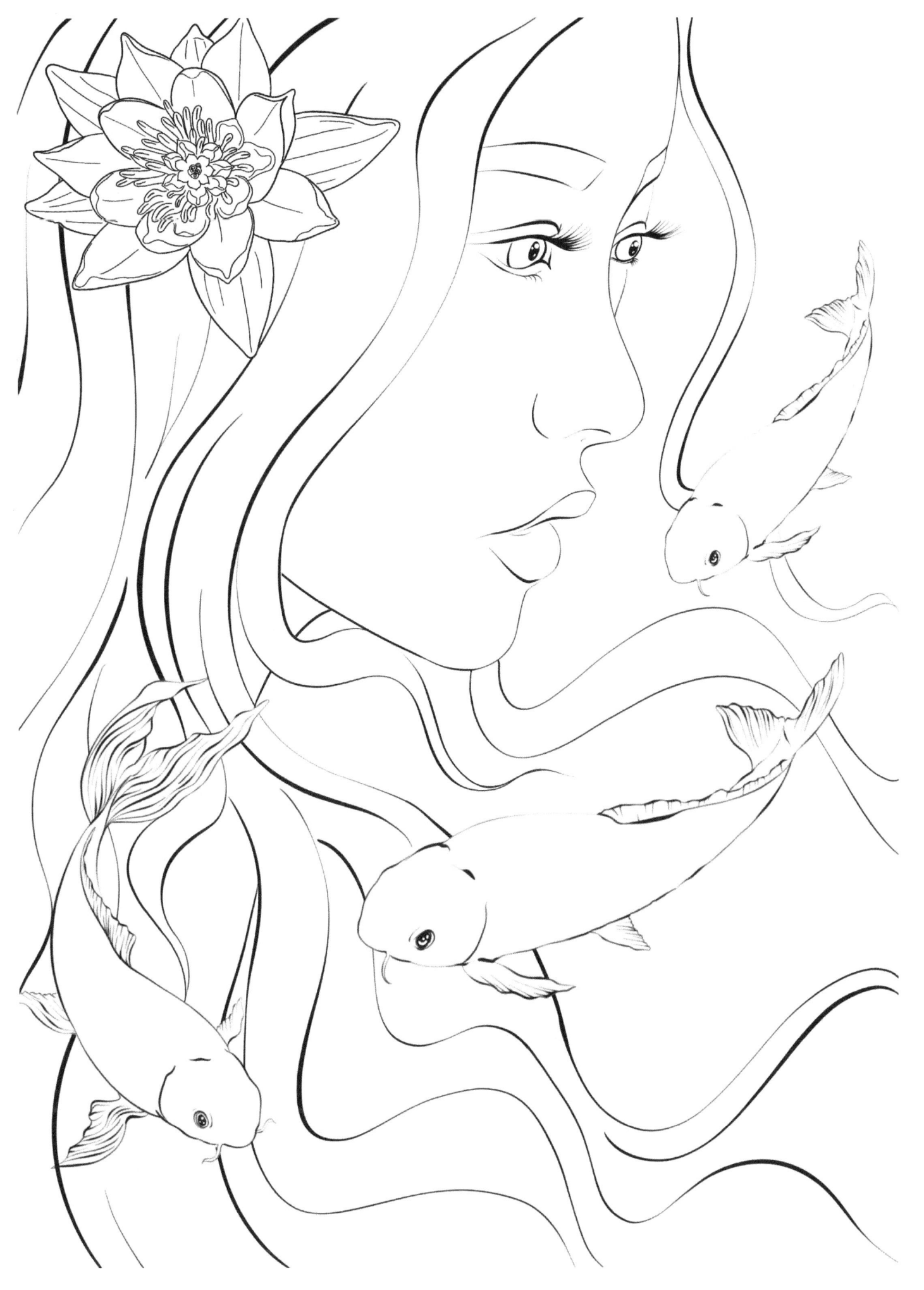

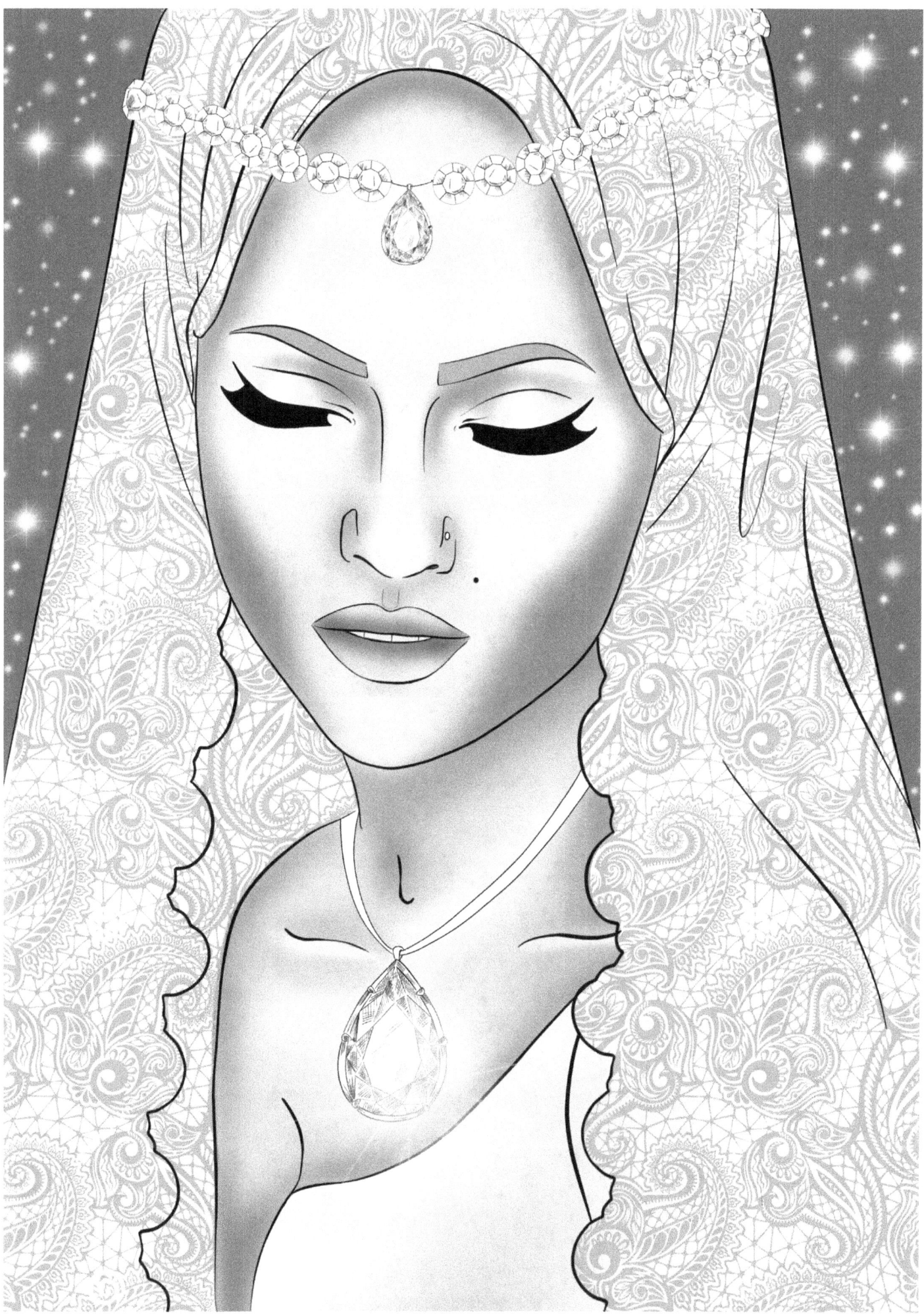

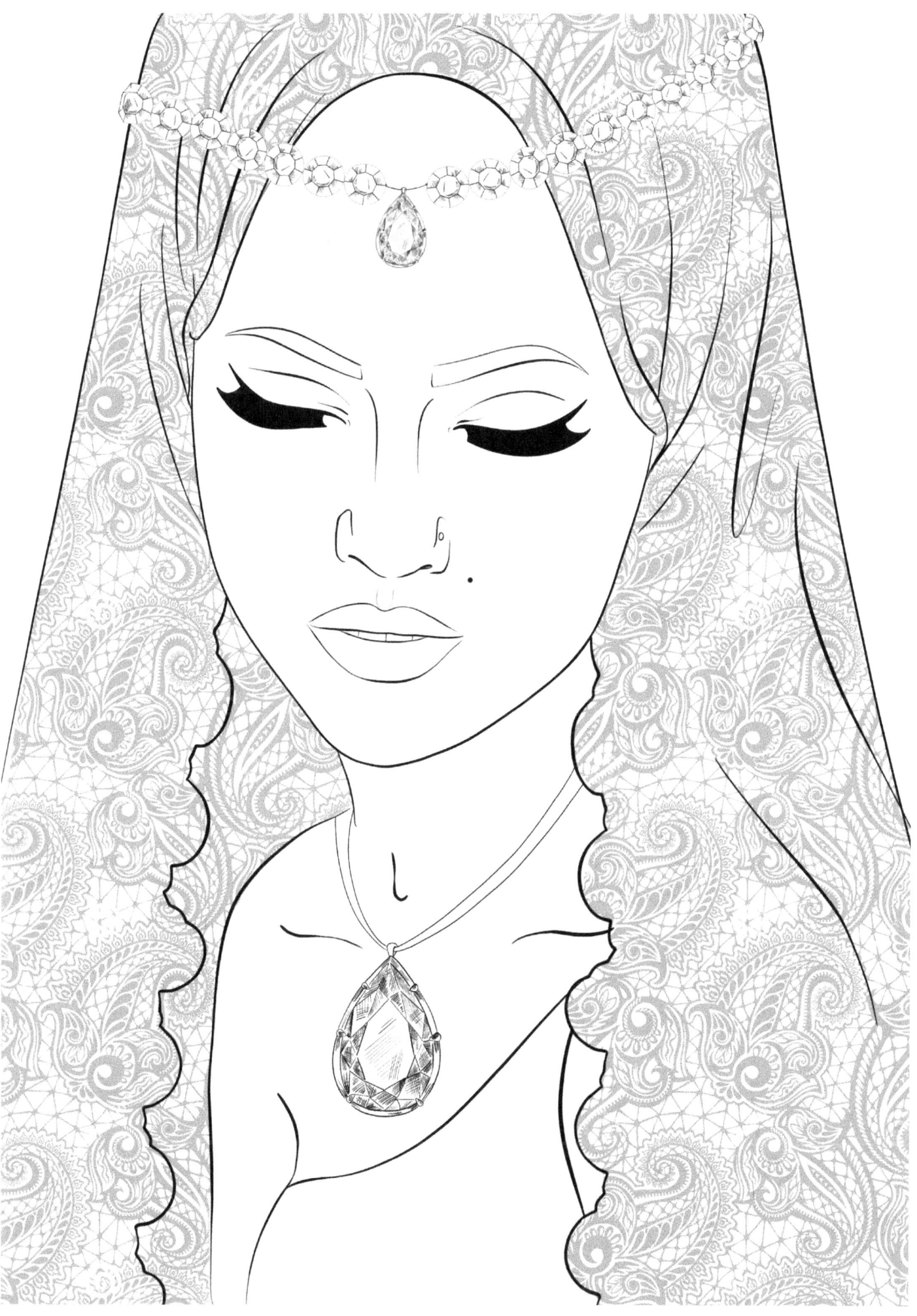

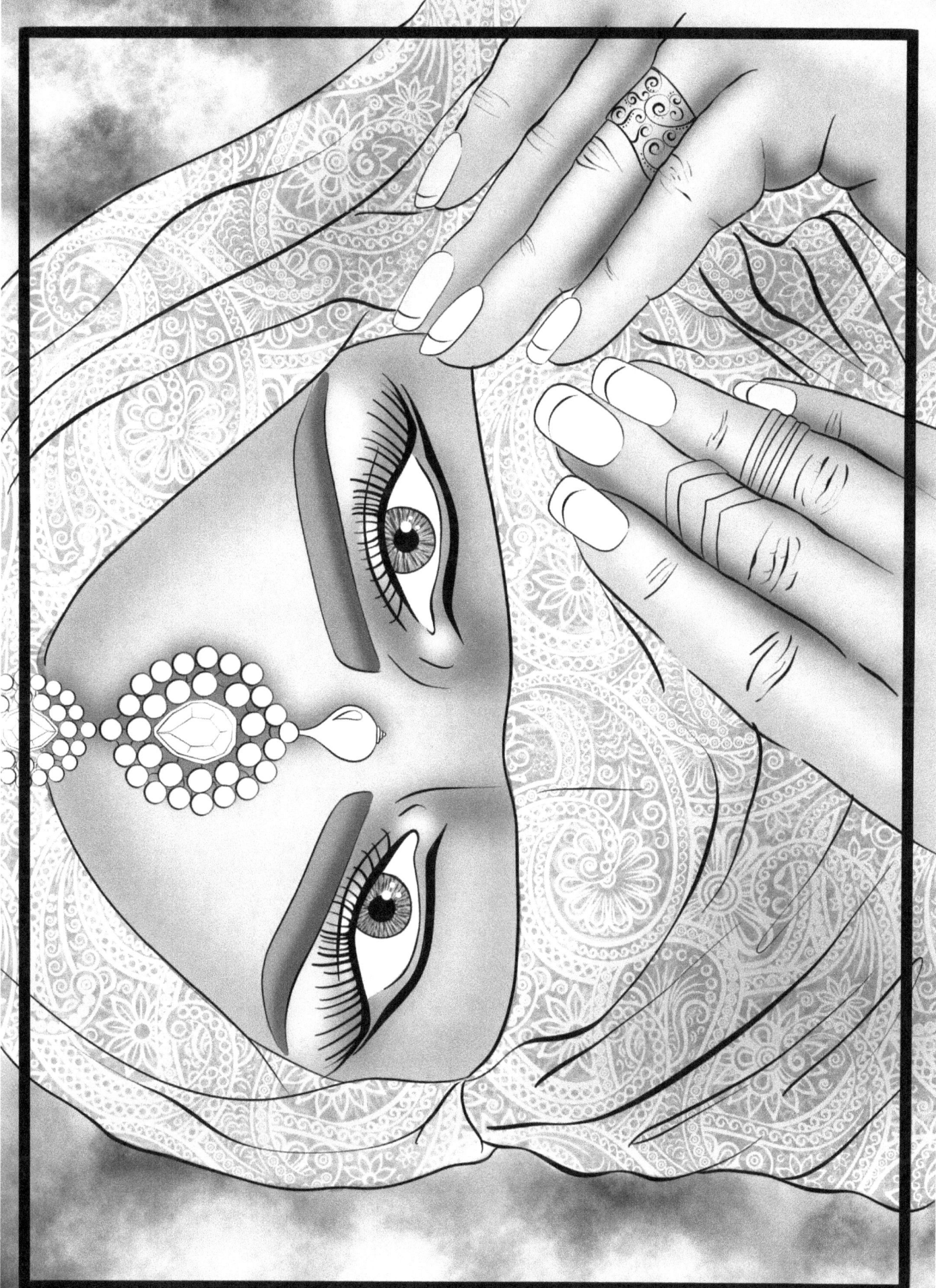

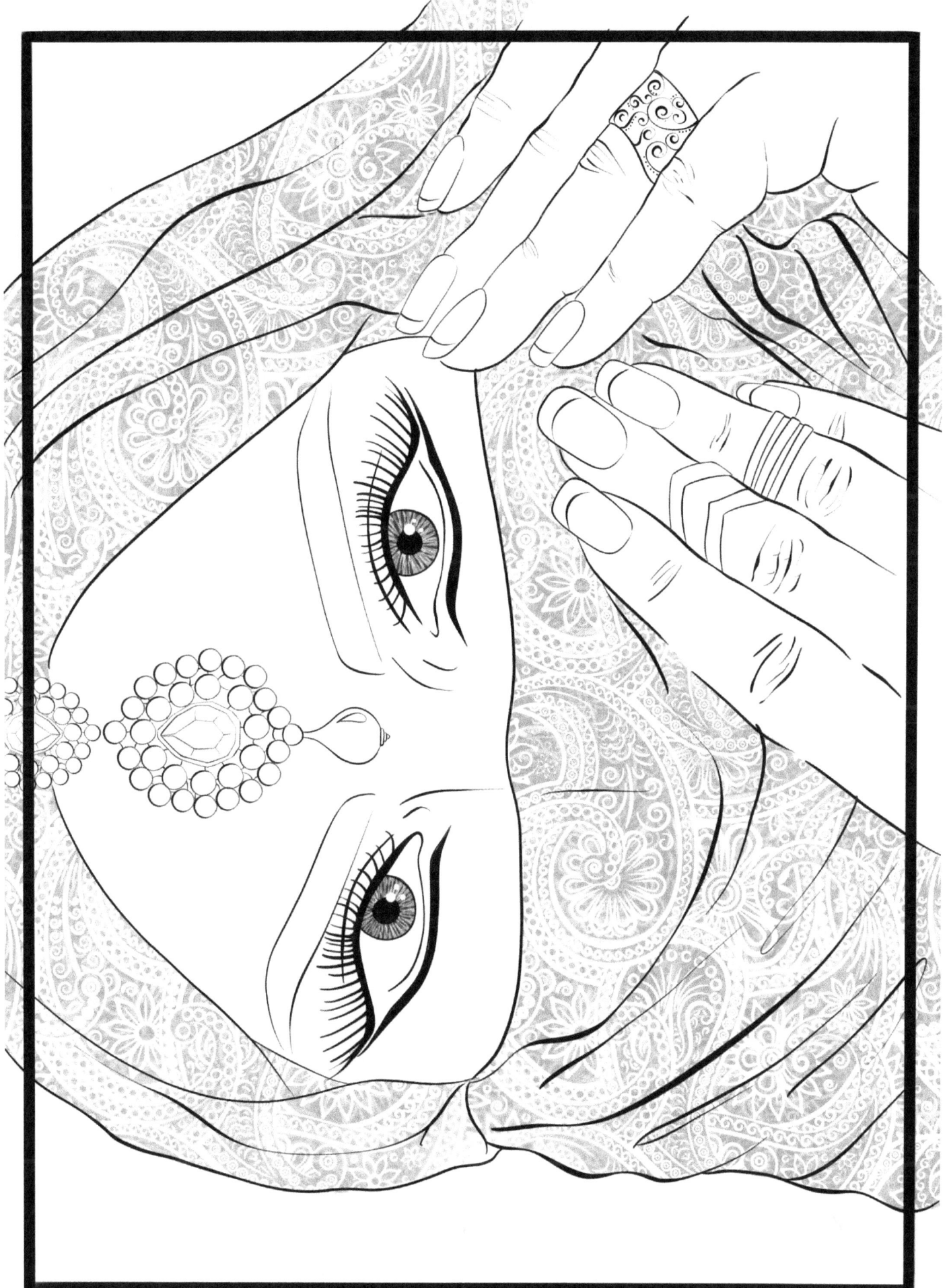

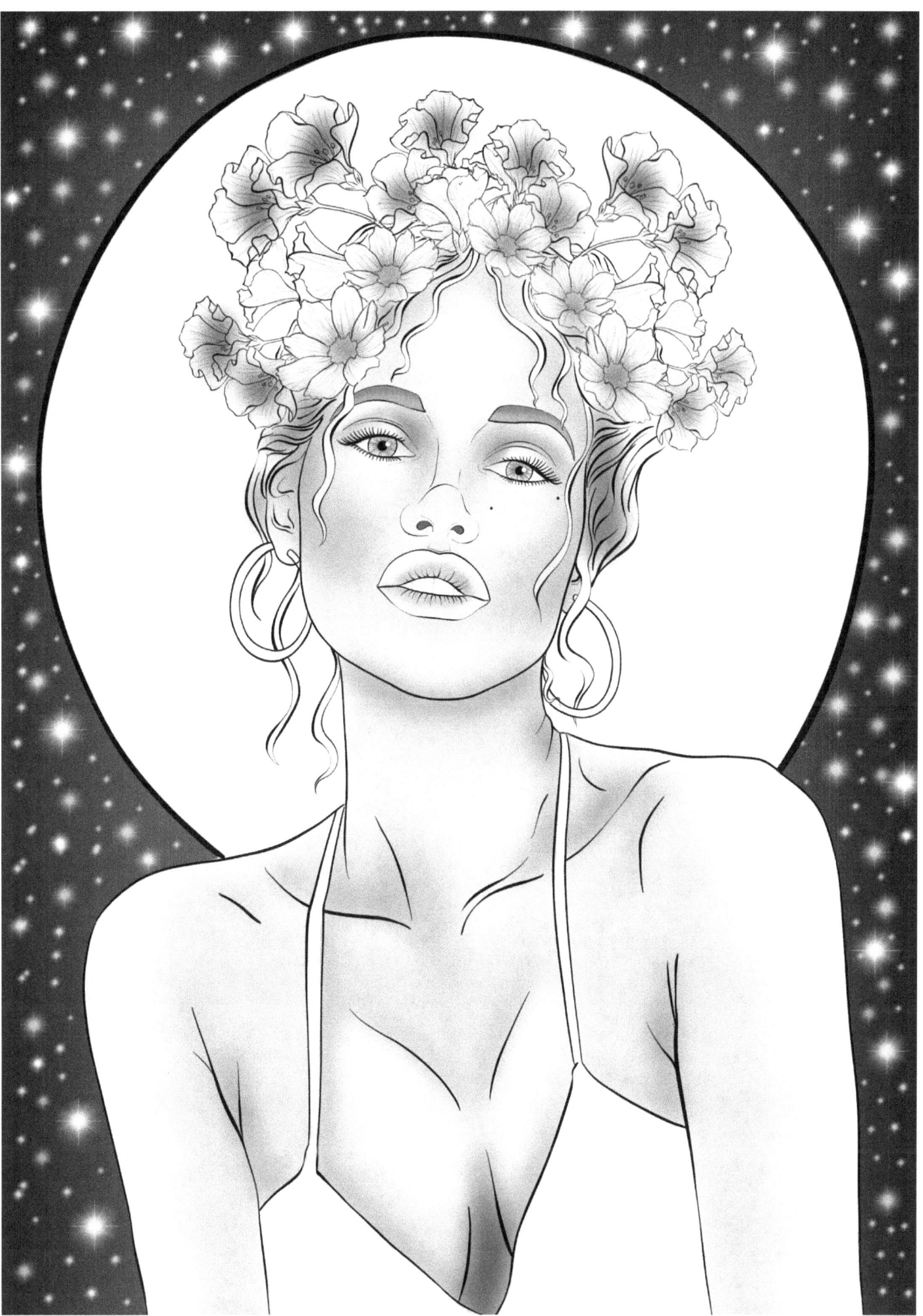

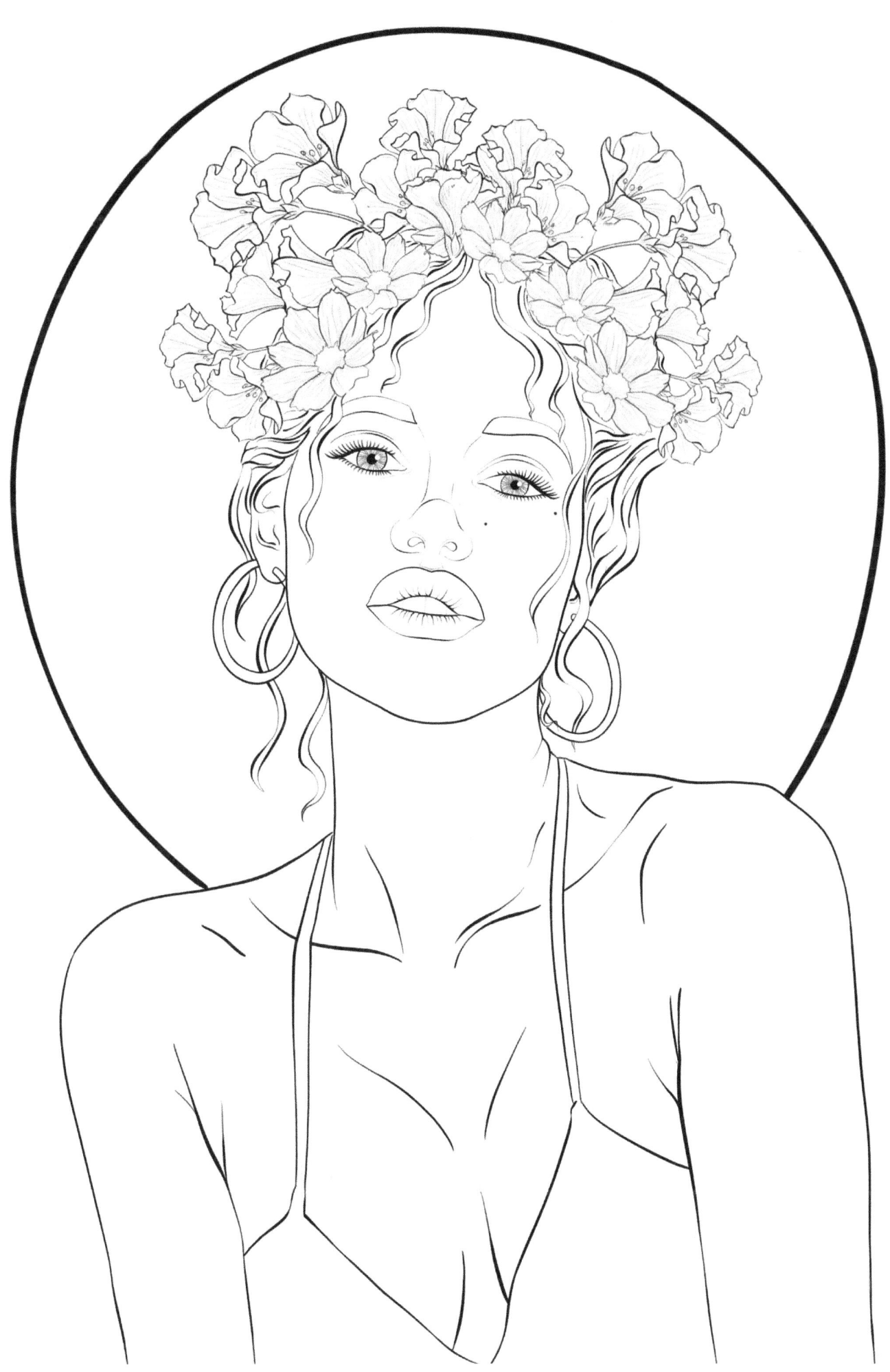

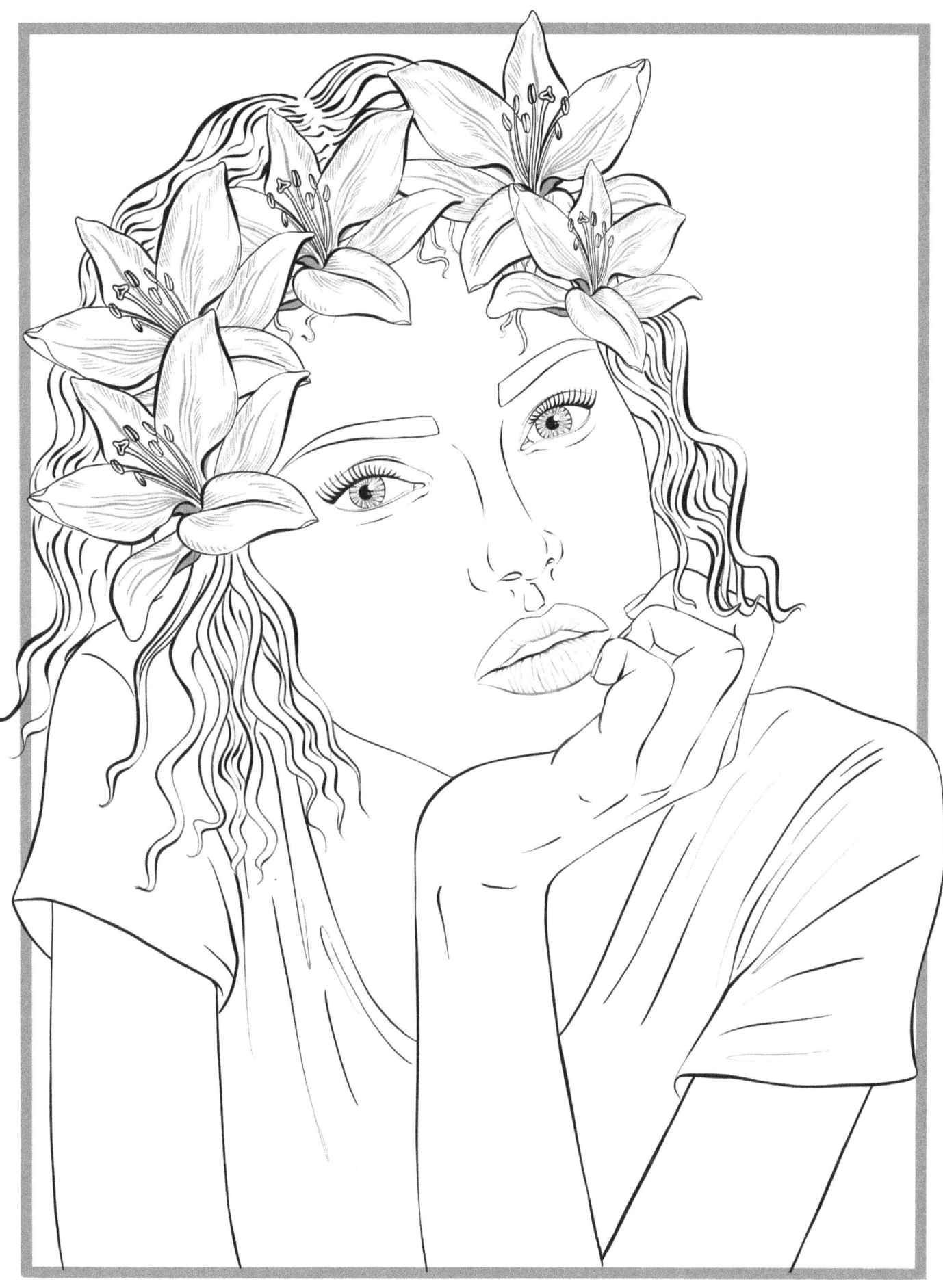

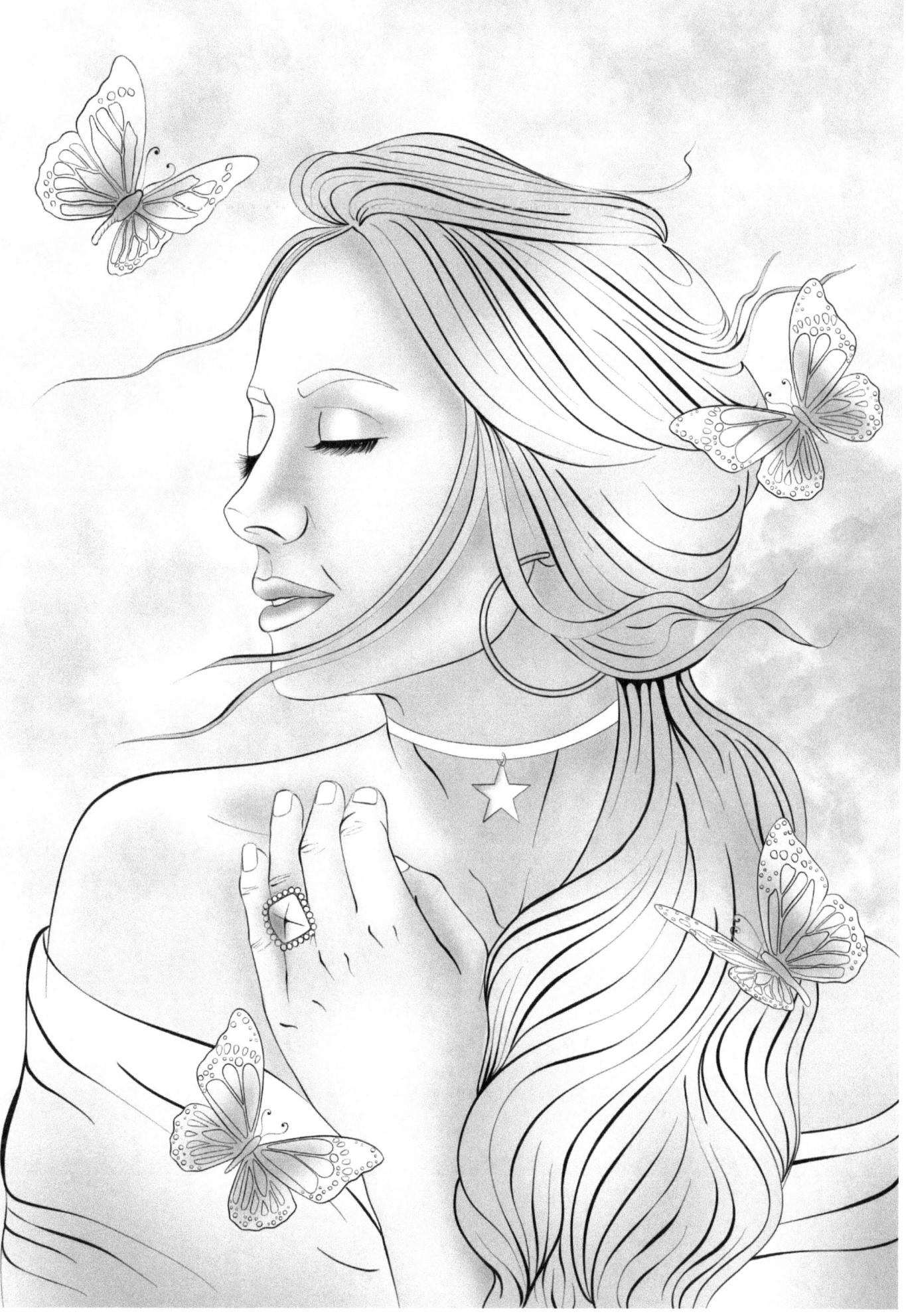

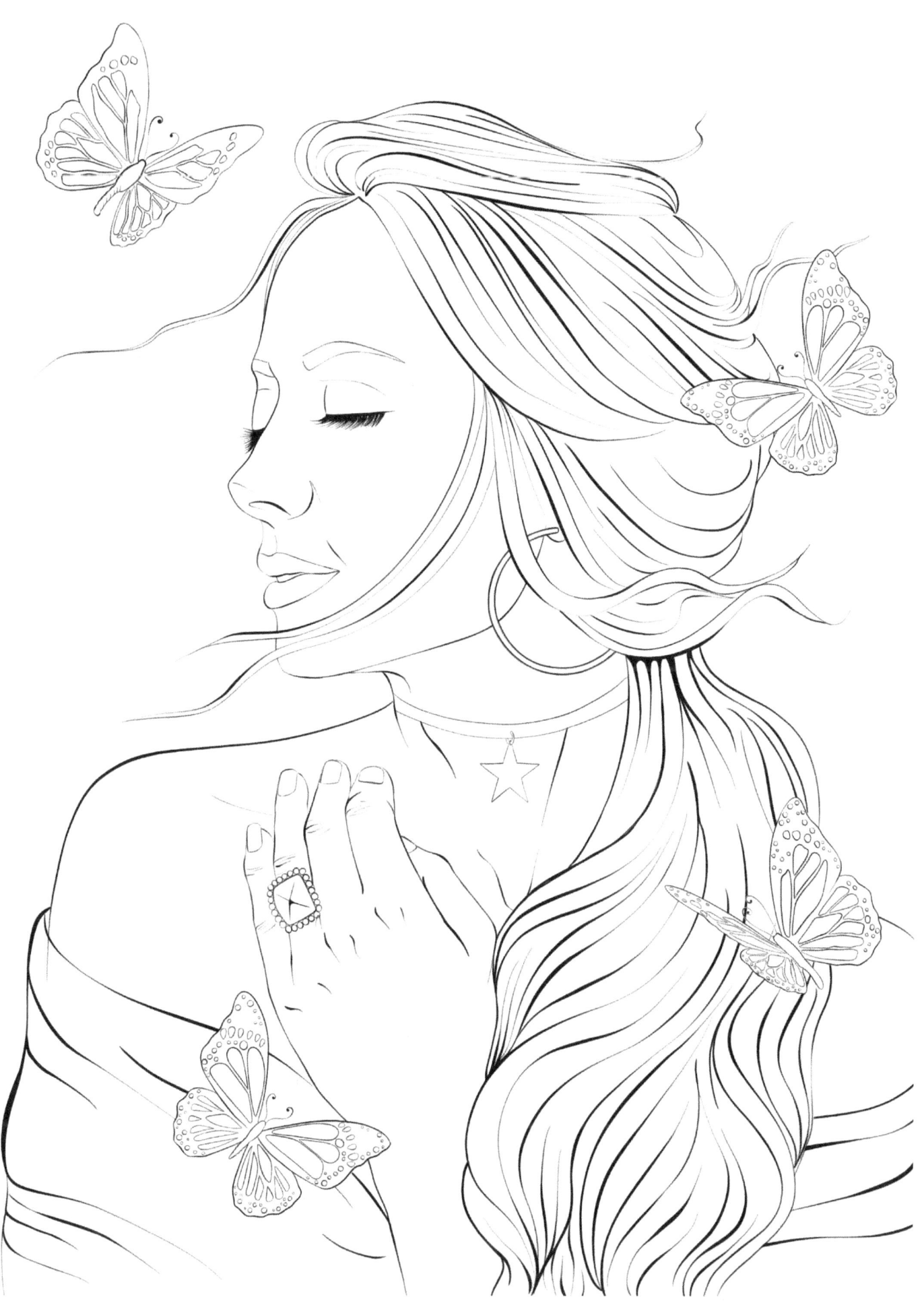

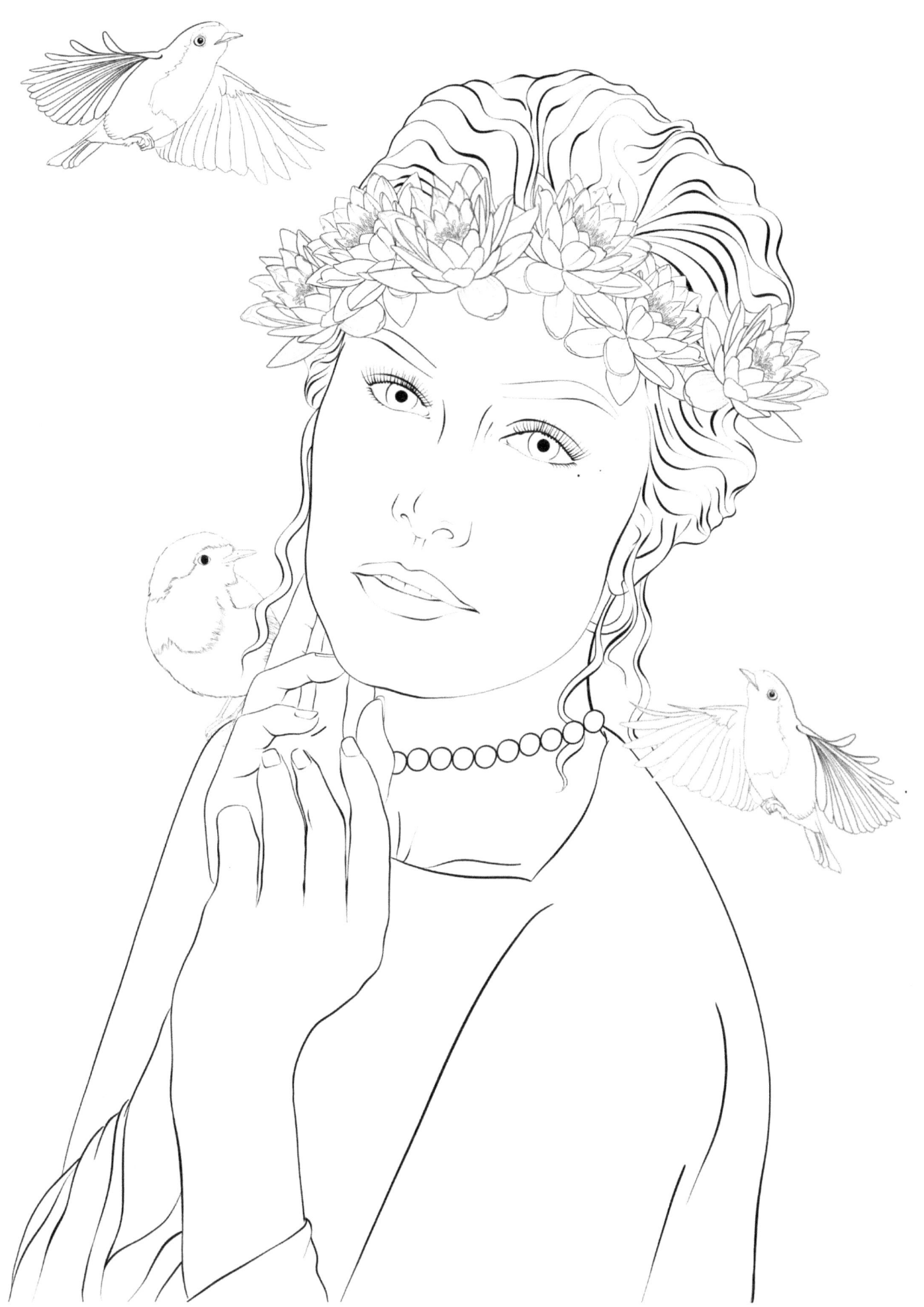

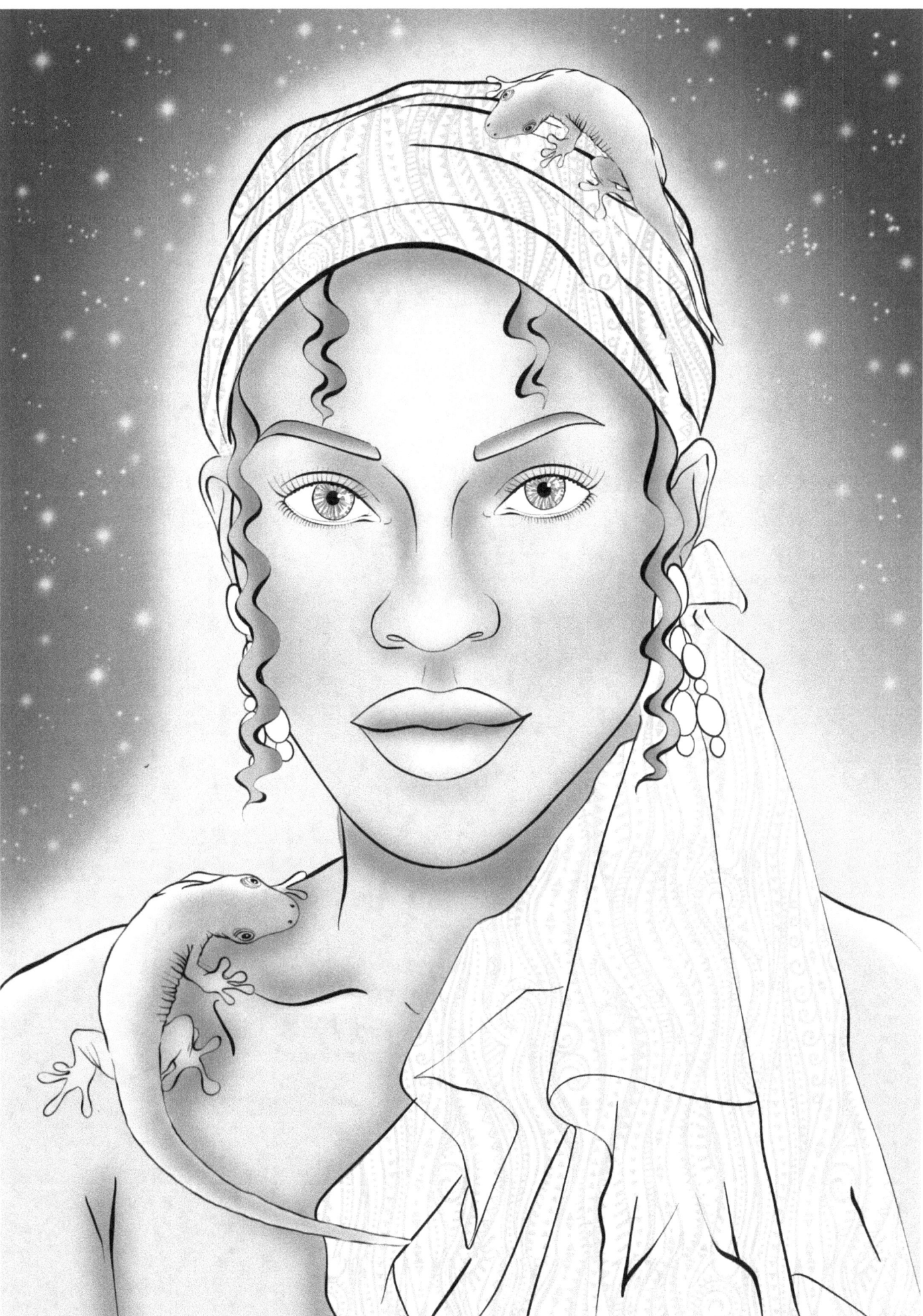

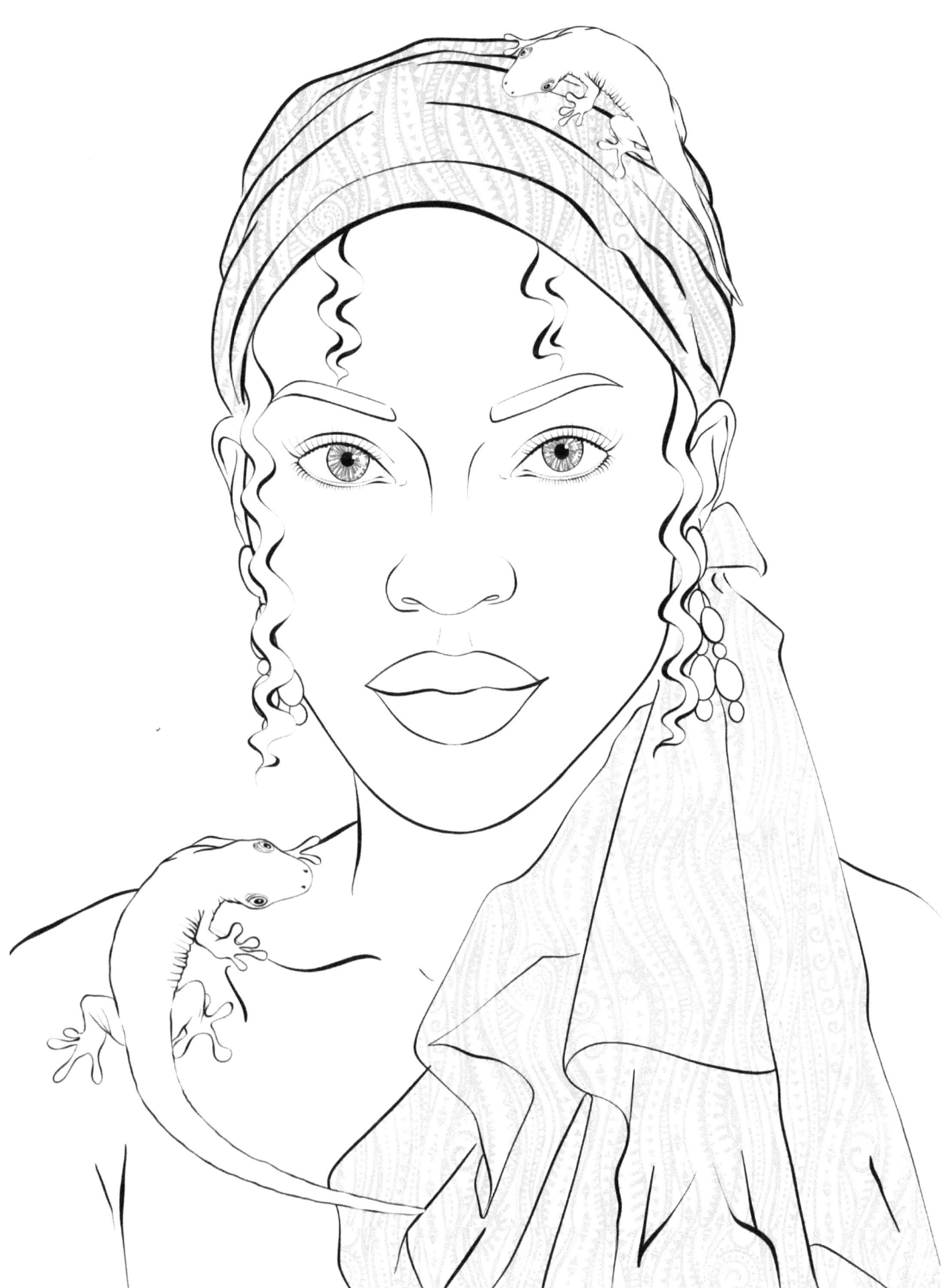

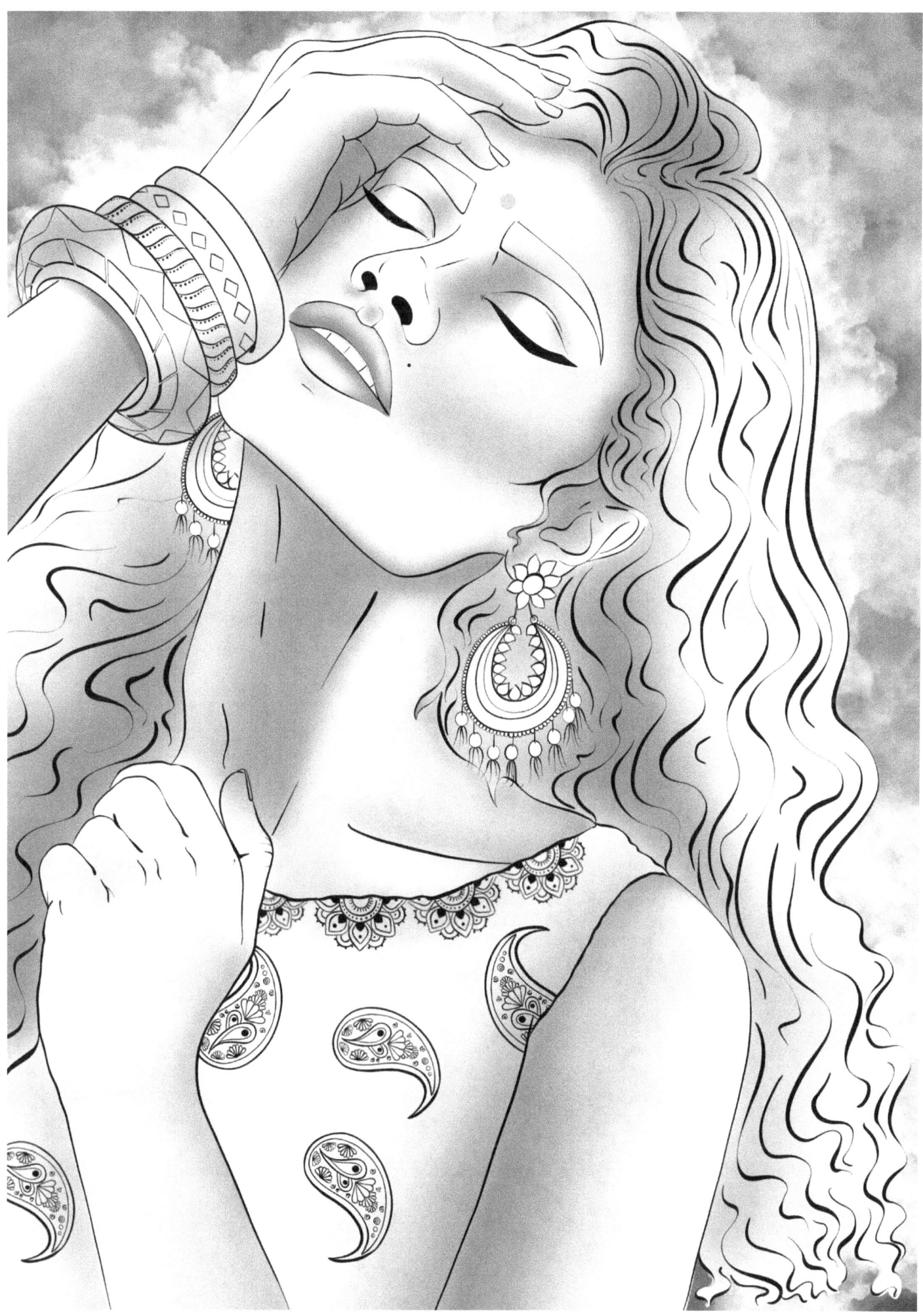

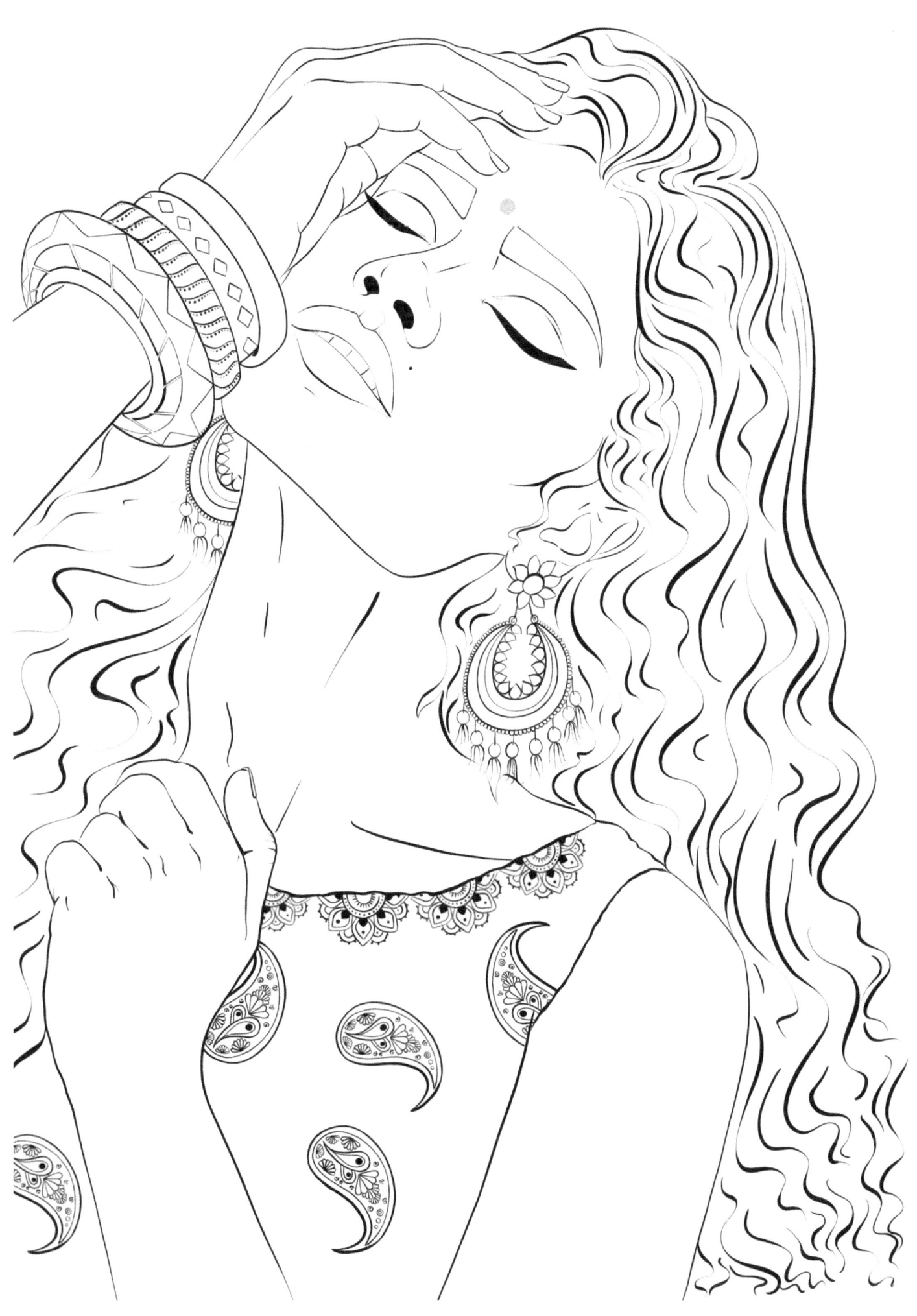

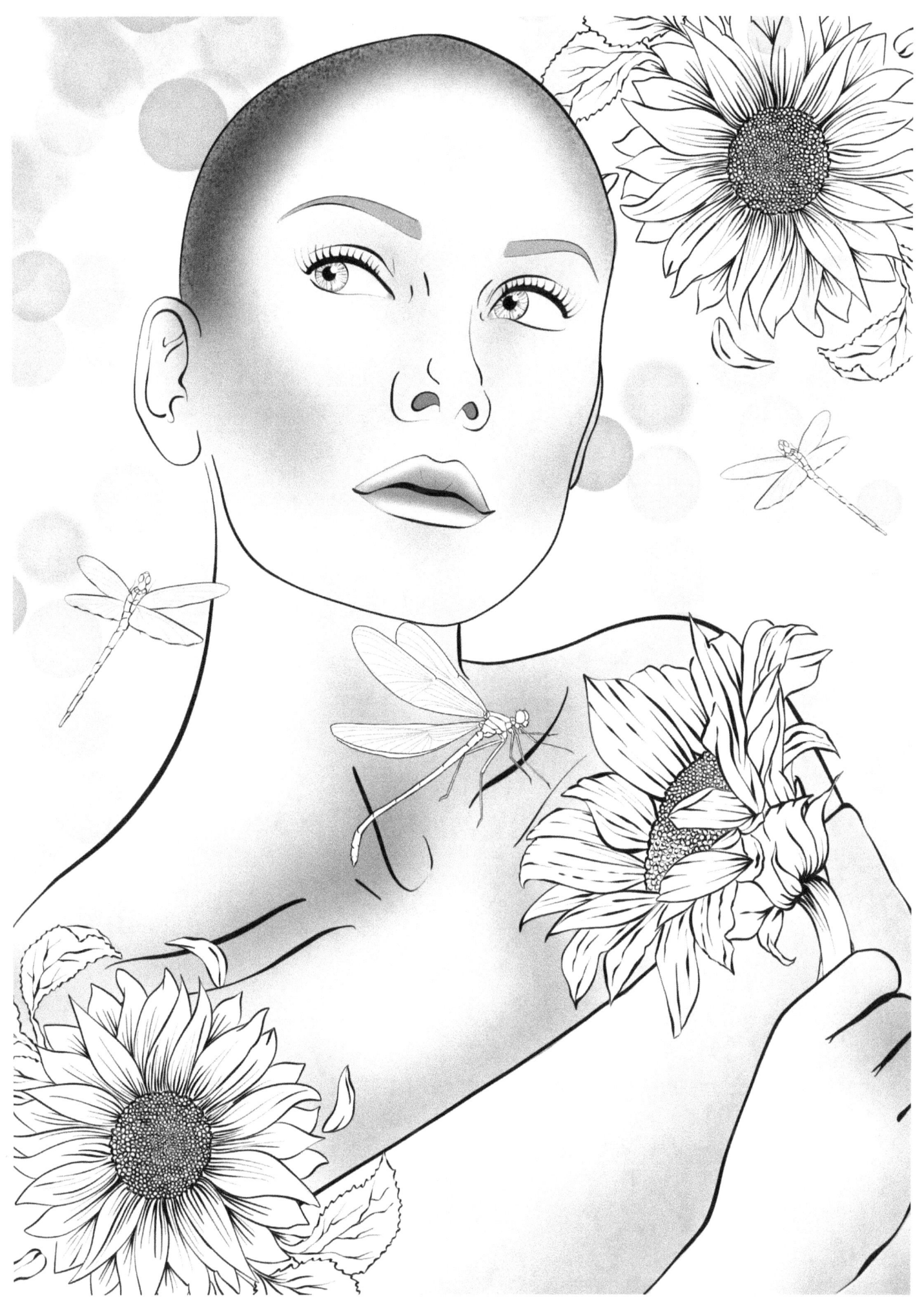

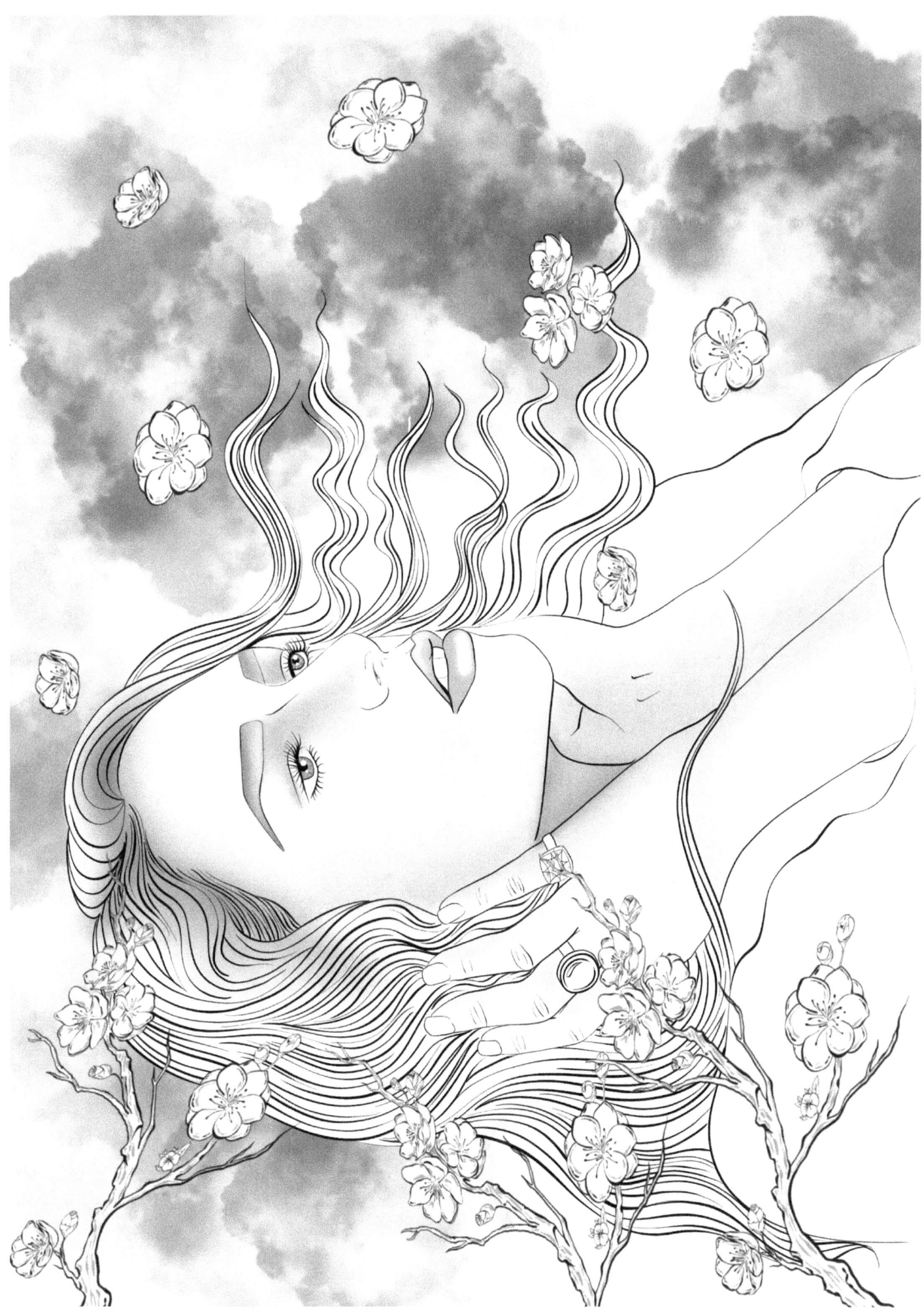

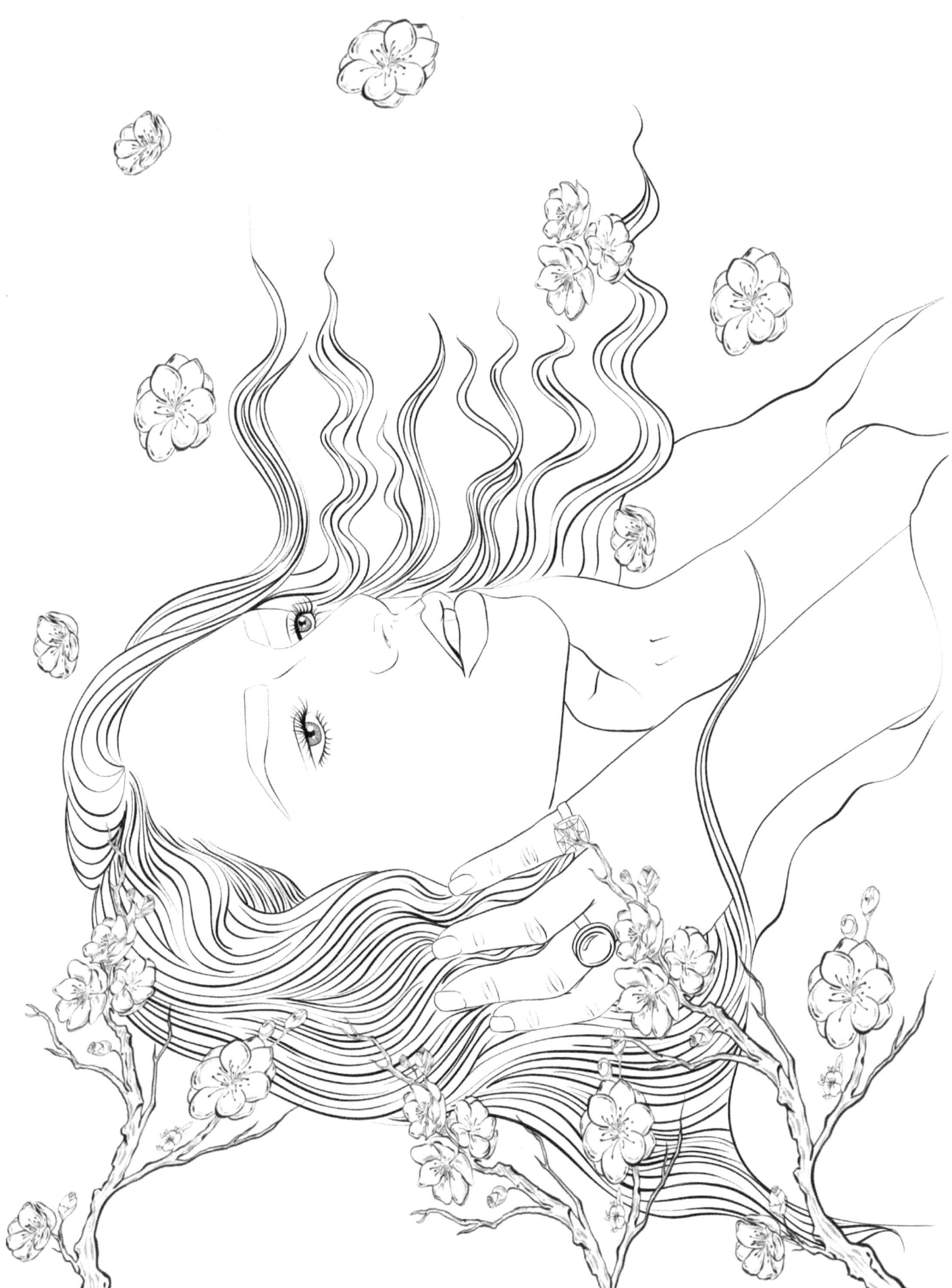